TEAM BUILDING
ON A TIGHT SCHEDULE

James H. Shonk

ISBN   9-781453-859407

TEAM BUILDING
ON A TIGHT SCHEDULE

James H. Shonk

PREFACE

The acceleration of change, the complexity of issues that organizations face, increased international competition, and instant 24/7 communication have all added to the need for rapid results.

Organizations are responding by relying on teams of people with varying expertise, in hopes that they can quickly resolve issues and bring new products and services to an ever-changing marketplace. However, there is seldom time for learning how to work as a team or to determine how to correct the dysfunctional actions of the team and the organization that make teams less than they can be.

Team Building is in response to this need for quick team results in an environment that allows little time for team training. It provides quick and effective methods to start up new teams and improve the performance of existing teams. Through the use of assessment tools, teams identify the issues that are keeping them from accomplishing their objectives. They use and learn effective team processes while resolving these issues.

Team Building is not a compilation of games. But, it is exciting and will keep your attention, because it deals with the work of your team and its problems.

You will use *Team Building* as a self-help method to accomplish real work and learn how to effectively interact. No trainer or facilitator is required unless you desire to have someone fill this role.

Each member of the team receives their own copy of *Team Building*. Pre-reading and the completion of assessment tools is required before each team building meeting.

Team Building can be used as a one day meeting, can be spread over several meetings, or applied as issues occur. Teams pick the issues they want to work on, eliminating issues of little value. The amount of time allocated depends upon the number and complexity of issues identified. The advantage of scheduling a one full day meeting is that the openness of communication increases as trust is built throughout the day. The advantage of several shorter meetings is that follow-up actions can be completed prior to the next meeting.

Action planning, follow-up responsibilities and a short team refresher meeting to ensure continuous improvement are built in.

BENEFITS

- Resolution of team identified issues

- Resolution of organizational issues affecting the team

- Clarification of and agreement to team goals and interdependencies

- Clarification of team members' roles and resolution of conflicts and overlaps.

- Improvement of team communications, decision making, meetings and conflict resolution.

- Improvement of working relationships

HOW TO MAKE IT WORK

Team Leaders

If you are not willing to share some of the decision making, allow the team to participate in setting goals, listen to others, encourage open communication, and perhaps change your role - do not undertake team building. The team will see your effort as a sham, or "business as usual", and you will not achieve the teamwork and improved performance desired.

Team Members

Team members must be willing to contribute with the best interests of the team in mind. Hidden agendas greatly diminish the team's ability to work together. Everyone must be willing to share their ideas and be open to the ideas of others.

TABLE OF CONTENTS

CHAPTER 1

EFFECTIVE TEAMS

Team Model

There are five factors that influence a team's effectiveness[1]. As a team, you will address each factor and determine if and what you need to do in each of these five areas to improve your performance. The first factor is the influence of the environment. Outside influences can have a major impact upon a team's effectiveness. The policies, systems and the structure of an organization can either support or hinder a team's effectiveness. For example, a recognition system that pits one person against another is not conducive to teamwork. An organization conducive to teamwork organizes teams around tasks that require coordination and provides appropriate resources. Outside demands from customers or lack of organizational support can influence the team's effectiveness. Managing environmental influences is the team's responsibility, but may require help from outside the team, such as a sponsor or key manager.

ENVIRONMENTAL: The impact of influences outside of the team

Policies/Procedures: Approval levels, Employment stability

Systems: Information, Financial reporting, Rewards

Organization Structure: Hierarchical, Flat or Organized by function or discipline or by teams.

Outside Demands: Customers, Government

Organization Support: Support from Key people, Resources allocated, Management expectations and time frames.

---

1 Ronald Fry and James Shonk. Unpublished material developed for a University of Michigan seminar on Team Development.

GOALS - What the team is to accomplish

A team exists when members have responsibility for accomplishing a common goal. However, many organizations form teams but continue to set goals individually, when in fact many of the individual goals should be team goals. Goals should have the following characteristics:

Clarity and Understanding

Unclear goals or differences in goal interpretation will lead team members in different directions and may result in conflict and little teamwork.

Ownership

The degree of goal ownership by all team members and the amount of energy expended toward achieving them are to a great extent determined by the amount of participation in creating them and determining how they will be accomplished.

Operational

Goals should be well defined, quantified if possible, and specific enough that members will know when they have accomplished them and can measure the result.

Shared Implementation Plans

It should be clearly understood by all members what others are planning to accomplish, the possible impact upon team members, and how their actions can help or hinder team members' contributions.

No Conflict

Occasionally, the goals of team members will be in conflict. The conflict must be resolved to ensure effective teamwork.

ROLES - Who does what on the team

Team members need to understand their roles and the roles of others and agree to them. The team will review their respective roles to ensure they meet the following criteria:

Clarity

The more interdependent the team, the more important it is that all members understand others' responsibilities as well as their own. This allows members to help each other and act more interchangeably.

Ownership and agreement

All members should know and agree upon the responsibilities of each member

No Conflict

Members' roles should complement one another rather than be conflicting. Role overlap can frequently be a source of conflict, as it is often unclear who does what or where one person's responsibilities end and the others begin.

Team Leader

Some teams rotate the leadership role. Others have permanent team leaders. The team should have input to determine the most appropriate leadership style based upon what the team's task requires. If there is a team leader, he/she must be open to feedback from team members regarding how their actions contribute to or detract from the team's effectiveness.

WORK PROCESS - How members work together

Once a team has established what they are to do and who will do it they need to determine how they will work together. The processes the team uses to perform work should be understood and agreed to.

Decision making:

Who will be responsible for decisions and how each of the team members participates in the decision must be clearly defined so that decisions are accepted and of high quality.

Communications:

Teams should determine what to communicate, to whom, by what methods, when, and how frequently.

Meetings:

Meetings should have an agenda that identifies the subjects to be covered and clearly defines what the team is to accomplish.

RELATIONSHIPS - The quality of interaction

Cause of Conflicts

As team members work together, conflicts can arise and relationships can become strained and affect the team's effectiveness. Members need ways to resolve problems and to assure that a good working relationship continues. Open communications during periodic teamwork assessments can help reduce such conflicts.

Conflicts are frequently rooted in one of the first four team effectiveness factors, and surface within the team as relationship problems. For example, the conflict could be the result of conflicting supervisory expectations, disagreement on the team goal, or lack of clarity regarding responsibilities or decision making authority.

When conflicts arise, the team should use the conflict resolution process outlined later in the program.

SUMMARY OF TEAM EFFECTIVENESS MODEL

ENVIRONMENTAL - The Impact of Outside Influences
- Policies and procedures
- Systems
- Organization structure
- Outside demands
- Expectations
- Organizational support

GOALS - What the Team is to Accomplish
- Clarity and understanding
- Ownership
- Operational
- Shared
- No conflicts

ROLES - Who does what
- Clarity
- Ownership and agreement
- Conflict

WORK PROCESSES - How Members Work Together
- Decision making
- Communications
- Meetings

RELATIONSHIPS - Quality of Interaction
- Conflict

HIERARCHY

Rubin, Fry, and Plovnick[2] found that these variables interact, that poor or good performance in one area can affect another. Furthermore, they found that there is a hierarchy of interactions for these variables.

Some variables were found to potentially influence all others. Those at the top of the hierarchy influence all below them. The team hierarchy can be depicted as follows:

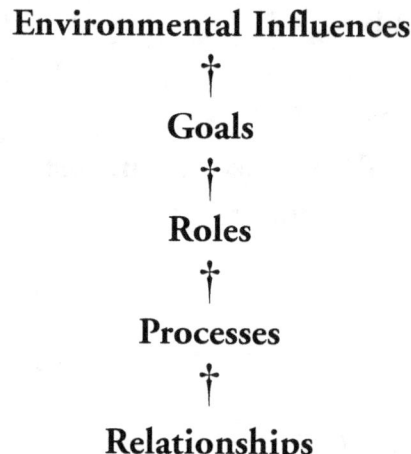

Environmental Influences

†

Goals

†

Roles

†

Processes

†

Relationships

This interactive influence can be illustrated by examples of problems commonly identified by teams and by examining the root causes of the problems. For example, requests for team development activity often start with two members of the team feeling they have a relationship problem. Experience has shown that often these members do not have a relationship problem outside of work; that is, they socialize well outside of the workplace. Closer examination reveals the root of the relationship problem is that they disagree on what the goal should be for the team, or they have conflicting roles, or one thinks the team should make decisions as a group and the other that each person should make decisions in his own area of responsibility. What appears to be a relationship problem may have another root cause and may in fact be a goal, role, or process issue.

Environmental influences sometimes put different and conflicting demands on mem-

2 Irwin M. Rubin, Ronald C. Fry, and Mark S. Plovnick, Managing Human Resources in Health Care Organizations: An Applied Approach. Reston, Va.; Reston Publishing Co. Inc. 1978.

bers of the team and can create relationship problems. On a multi-disciplined project team, where members report to different functional heads, the conflicting expectations of the multiple bosses may lead to team conflict, which is manifested and diagnosed as a relationship problem. The root cause, however, is the conflicting multiple demands.

When one member of a team sees the goal as X and another as Y, it becomes obvious why they always argue during team meetings. Properly diagnosed, this is a goal problem, and if the team attempts to solve it by improving the relationship between the two parties, you are working at the wrong level of the team hierarchy. Similarly, role problems may be the result of poor understanding or definition of the goal.

Therefore, what appears to be a problem at one level of the hierarchy may have its root cause at a higher level. When in doubt as to where the problem exists, first look at the higher-level variables to determine what, in fact, is causing the problem, before you attempt to solve the problem at the level where the symptoms first appear.

As a team you will address each of the five areas of the Team Effectiveness model and determine what can be done to make the team more effective.

Characteristics of Effective and Ineffective Teams

Data collected over a three year period at The University of Michigan during team development seminars asked participants: What are the characteristics of effective and ineffective teams? Responses to these questions were catalogued, using the team hierarchy. A sample array of responses follows.

Instructions: If there are items on this list that seem relevant to your team, make a note of them and bring them up for further discussion at the point in the program that covers the general topic, e.g. goals or roles.

EFFECTIVE TEAMS	INEFFECTIVE TEAMS
Environment	**Environment**
Team members are in close physical proximity and able to meet regularly.	Physical separation prevents members from meeting frequently.
The appropriate skills are represented on the team.	Team is not given adequate resources.
	There is no recognition of team effort.
The appropriate levels of organizational authority are present within the team.	There is a lack of recognition by the organization or its leaders that a team exists.
Goals	**Goals**
Team members are involved in the setting of objectives.	Members do not participate in setting goals.
Objectives are understood by all members.	Goals are unclear
	Goals are not communicated.
Objectives are set and met within realistic time frames.	Everyone is doing his/her own thing without attention to team goals.

EFFECTIVE TEAMS

Roles

Roles are clearly defined and do not overlap.

Team members and the leader know their responsibilities

Roles are understood and supported.

There is effective leadership with clearly defined responsibilities.

Members and leader help each other.

Processes

Decisions are made by consensus.

Meetings are efficient and work-improvement oriented

Emphasis is on solving problems, versus blaming the individual responsible for the problem.

All members participate in discussions and meetings.

Minutes of meetings are promptly distributed.

Members listen well

INEFFECTIVE TEAMS

Roles

Responsibilities are poorly defined.

No clear leadership responsibilities are identified.

There is buck-passing of responsibility

Members engage in power plays for authority and control.

Members refuse to recognize their interdependence and act as if they are independent.

Processes

Decisions are always a crisis situation.

Decision making is dominated by one person.

Communications are one way - from top down - and channeled through the leader.

Minor points are debated endlessly.

Meetings are unproductive, with the issues unresolved.

Meetings cover trivia, versus significant issues.

Characteristics of Effective and Ineffective Teams (cont.)

EFFECTIVE TEAMS	INEFFECTIVE TEAMS
There is frequent feedback.	Actions are taken without planning.
All members are kept informed.	Members work individually and ignore each other.
Deadlines and milestones are clearly established and agreed to by team.	Members are late for meetings or do not attend.

Relationships

Relationships

There is team identify or esprit de corps and pride.	Members are unwilling to be identified with the team.
There is tolerance for conflict, with an emphasis upon resolution.	There is covert conflict between members.
Conflict is openly discussed, often resulting in growth, or learning.	There are severe personality conflicts.
Members enjoy each other.	Relationships are competitive.
Team members support each other.	Members are defensive.

This book will supply you with the information, assessment tools, and processes to help you improve the team's performance in the previous five areas.

CHAPTER 2

HOW TO USE THIS BOOK

Team Building Preparation

The sequence of events for team building meetings generally contain the following steps.

PreWork

A. Individual reading to prepare for the meeting.

B. Individually completing assessment questionnaires.

C. Establishing an agenda for the team meeting, based upon the questionnaires or tasks. Some chapters have tasks for the team to perform rather than questionnaires to complete.

Team Meeting

A. Review of agenda for understanding and agreement.

B. Issue identification, problem solving and action planning.

C. Critique of meeting processes and outcomes and identification of agenda items for the next meeting.

The amount of time allocated for your meetings will depend upon the number of topics to be covered and their complexity. While you are meeting, keep in mind that there are two goals. The first is to do something, e.g issue identification or problem solving to improve the team's performance toward accomplishing the team's objectives. Second is to learn how to work more effectively as a team.

New Teams

Team development can be helpful when new teams are formed. The team hierarchy can serve as a road map to ensure that the team gets off on the right foot.

New teams should start with a kick-off meeting, during which everyone hears what the reasons are for establishing the team. The specific agenda for the meeting should cover the following subjects.

AGENDA - NEW TEAM KICK-OFF MEETING

Goals
• Why this team was created
• Team mission
• Team goals (to extent established)
• Limitations to the team's scope

Environmental Influences
• Organization support, budget, manpower, etc.
• Potential roadblocks to accomplishing the team's tasks
• Outside competition (if relevant) and its impact on the team
• Rewards for team goals
• Limitations or constraints

Roles
• Introduction of members
• Why certain functions or departments are, or are not represented
• Members' responsibilities (to extent defined)
• Support staff needed and their availability

Processes
• Team decision making authority (to extent defined)
• The organization's communications expectations to and from the team
• Where to go for help

Questions and Answers

_____

_____

_____

_____

_____

_____

_____

FIRST TEAM-BUILDING MEETING

The first team building meeting should take place approximately two weeks after the kick-off meeting. This gives the team enough time and history to understand what they need to work on to effectively accomplish their goals. Because new teams have little history together they may need to answer the assessment questionnaires according to how they want the team to function.

Existing Teams

Existing teams should proceed with their team building meeting the first date they can meet with total team attendance.

The number of subjects or chapters covered will depend on the time allocated and number of issues to discuss. Where there is total agreement that the team is functioning well, there is usually little benefit in further discussion. Team time should be concentrated on areas where there is room for improvement.

CHAPTER 3

HOW INTERDEPENDENT ARE WE?

Team Definition

A team consists of two or more people who must coordinate their activities to accomplish a common task.[3] The common goal or task and the coordination required determine whether a team exists. If members depend on each others' work or services, make joint decisions, supply each other with resources or share common resources, they are a team. If the work does not require coordination there is no team.

Team Interdependence

Interdependence is the extent to which team members depend on each other or need to coordinate their activities to accomplish the team's goals. The nature of the task determines the amount of coordination/interdependence required to accomplish it. For example, assembly line operations which tend to be low in interdependence can best be exemplified by a relay racing team. Their interdependence is sequential and at the point of the hand-off of the baton. During the majority of the race team members perform their tasks independently of each other. Members cannot help each other by running part of the race for them. However, some organizations have replaced low interdependent assembly operations with more highly interdependent teams.

A team that represents high interdependence between its members is a basketball team. Their interdependence is mutual. They can help each other out, they must coordinate their actions constantly and they are interchangeable. They can switch positions and take turns passing, shooting, and rebounding.

3 Plovnick, Fry, and Rubin. "New Developments in O.D. Technology: Programmed Team Development," Training and Development Journal, April 4, 1975

Team members may have different expectations about how closely they should coordinate their activities. The team interdependence questionnaire is designed to help the team determine and agree on the appropriate level of team member interdependence.

To determine your team's optimum level of interdependence, complete the Team Interdependence Questionnaire. As you complete it, keep in mind the team's goals. If goals do not exist, the team should complete the goals section and then do the interdependence questionnaire.

Team Interdependence Questionnaire

Purpose: To determine the degree of team member interdependence and therefore, the extent of coordination required to accomplish the team's work.

Instructions: Each member of the team should complete this questionnaire by placing an **N** *above the number for the statement that best describes the team now, and an* **F** *above the statement that is most desirable for the future. List in the comments section some recent examples that illustrate your choice. As a team, discuss your responses and determine the appropriate level of interdependence and document any actions required to reach that level. Apply the Meeting Guidelines (to follow) during this and all future meetings.*

GOALS

1	2	3
Goals are separate	Some shared responsibility for goals	Many common goals

Comments: _____

_____

_____

ROLES

1	2	3
Individuals are responsible for accomplishing their goals	Sub groups of the team are responsible for accomplishing goals	Team is responsible for accomplishing goals

Comments: _____

_____

_____

RESOURCES

1	2	3
Members have their own resources	Members share some common resources	The team shares many common resources

Comments: _____

_____

_____

IMPLEMENTATION

1	2	3
Work can be accomplished most effectively by working alone	Work can be accomplished effectively by some members coordinating their activities	Work can be accomplished most effectively by all members coordinating their activities

Comments: _____

_____

_____

PLANNING

1	2	3
Planning and progress feedback is done individually	Planning and progress feedback is done in subgroups	Planning and progress feedback is done by the team

Comments: _____

_____

_____

COMMUNICATIONS

1	2	3
Members communicate one on one	Subgroups communicate	Communications are a team responsibility

Comments: _____

_____

_____

MEETINGS

1	2	3
Few team meetings Mostly one on one	Periodic team meetings	Frequent team meetings

Comments: _____

_____

_____

DECISIONS

1	2	3
Decisions are made individually and do not impact the work of others	Decisions are made by the people impacted	Decisions are made by consensus and impact the work of most

Comments: _____

_____

_____

TIME FRAME

1	2	3
Members work for months before coordination is needed	Coordination is needed weekly or monthly	Activities must be coordinated on a daily or weekly basis

Comments: _____

_____

_____

Team Meeting Guidelines

A few general guidelines can greatly increase the effectiveness of a meeting. Select a leader, recorder, and if needed, a facilitator to help the leader keep the meeting on track. Use the following guidelines during all team meetings.

Establish an Agenda and Stick to it

When new subjects are raised, put them on a list to be discussed later. This will reduce topic jumping. It assures the person who has raised the subject that it will be addressed at a future time.

Listen to Others

Only one person should be talking at a time.

Paraphrase - if you are unsure of what has been said, check your understanding by briefly restating what you heard.

Use a note pad to jot down your thoughts or questions that arise as others are talking. Then you can continue to listen to others and be assured that you will not forget the point you wanted to make.

Use a Flip Chart or Computer Screen to Record Actions

Recording actions where all can see provides a focal point for everyone's attention. It allows the group to see where it is going, what it has accomplished and to refer back to points previously made.

Encourage Participation

Everyone should be encouraged to participate. Ask each member to give a "snapshot" - a 20 second comment on the subject being discussed.

Summarize and Test for Agreement

The meeting leader should summarize the proposed action. If it requires consensus, ask all members of the team if they agree or are willing to go along with the decision. If there is not general agreement, continue the discussion until there is reasonable support.

Clarify Follow-up Responsibilities

The meeting leader should ensure that someone assumes the responsibility to implement and/or follow-up on decisions.

MEETING RESPONSIBILITIES

Leader:
- State the purpose of the meeting.
- Assign facilitator and recorder responsibilities.
- Review agenda for additions or corrections.
- Reinforce meeting guidelines.
- Ensure decisions are reached and follow-up responsibilities are clear
- Conduct evaluation of meeting.
- Follow-up to ensure assignments are completed prior to next meeting.

Facilitator:
If the team chooses to have a facilitator for their meeting, the facilitator helps the team and the leader manage the meeting's process. He/she does not usurp the leader's role, but helps the team adhere to the meeting guidelines. This role should rotate so that all team members are conscious of the flow of your meetings.

Participant:
An effective meeting requires a team effort. Participant responsibilities are to:
- Submit agenda items for the meeting.
- Do prework and come prepared.
- Arrive on time.
- Participate fully by giving ideas and helping others to understand them.

- Follow and help reinforce meeting guidelines.
- Complete agreed to follow-up actions.

Recorder

At the beginning of each meeting, a recorder should be identified to keep a running summary. The flip chart or computer is a convenient tool for this. It provides a record of the meeting and also helps to focus the group's attention. Written or typed minutes that emphasize decisions made, actions required and team member responsibilities should be reproduced and distributed shortly after the meeting.

CHAPTER 4

DETERMINING YOUR TEAM'S EFFECTIVENESS

Use the material in this chapter to determine how effective your team functions and where there is opportunity for improvement. Individually complete the Team Effectiveness Questionnaire.

Team Effectiveness Questionnaire

Instructions: Complete this questionnaire and discuss team members' responses to determine how to improve team performance. "No" responses are areas for team discussion and the development of plans for improvement. One "no" response requires that the respondent's concerns be addressed. The results from this questionnaire will determine the subjects you discuss as a team as your proceed through this program. As a team, identify the major issues to be addressed as you continue through this book. For example: Chapter 5 covers how to deal with environmental influences.

ENVIRONMENT   **YES**   **NO**

1. The team is adequately managing outside influences.   ——   ——

2. The organization is adequately supporting the team.   ——   ——

3. Outside influences are positively affecting the team performance.   ——   ——

4. The time frame for our work is appropriate.   ——   ——

Comments: _____

_____

_____

GOALS	**YES**	**NO**
5. The team's mission is clear and agreed upon.	⎯⎯	⎯⎯
6. Team goals are clear, measurable and agreed upon.	⎯⎯	⎯⎯
7. Team members' goals are not in conflict.	⎯⎯	⎯⎯
8. Team members are committed to the team's goals.	⎯⎯	⎯⎯

Comments: _____
_____
_____

ROLES	**YES**	**NO**
9. Team members' roles are clear and agreed to.	⎯⎯	⎯⎯
10. Team members' roles are not in conflict.	⎯⎯	⎯⎯
11. Team members are performing their roles effectively.	⎯⎯	⎯⎯
12. There is effective use of team members' unique skills.	⎯⎯	⎯⎯
13. Assignments are finished on time.	⎯⎯	⎯⎯
14. The leader's role is effective for optimum team performance.	⎯⎯	⎯⎯

Comments: _____
_____
_____

PROCESSES	**YES**	**NO**
15. Decision making authority and the processes are clear.	⎯⎯	⎯⎯

PROCESSES (cont.)   YES   NO

16. The team uses consensus decision making when appropriate.   ———   ———

17. Decisions are made within the time deadlines.   ———   ———

18. The team consistently uses open dialogue and feedback.   ———   ———

19. The team receives the information it needs.   ———   ———

20. Team members are practicing active listening.   ———   ———

21. All meetings have an agenda.   ———   ———

22. Meetings consistently follow the agenda.   ———   ———

23. All members participate in meetings.   ———   ———

24. Meetings guidelines are followed.   ———   ———

25. Meetings are effective and cover relevant topics.   ———   ———

26. Meeting preparation and follow-up are consistently done.   ———   ———

27. Meetings are evaluated and improvements implemented.   ———   ———

28. Everyone who is needed at meetings always attends.   ———   ———

29. A clear plan exists for continually improving performance.   ———   ———

Comments: _____

_____

_____

RELATIONSHIPS   YES   NO

30. Relationships among team members are optimum.   ———   ———

31. Conflicts are quickly surfaced and resolved.   ———   ———

32. There are no conflicts within the team hurting our performance. ———   ———

Comments: _____

_____

_____

GENERAL

33. What is causing stress for the team?

Comments: _____

_____

_____

34. What will increase the effectiveness of the team?

Comments: _____

_____

_____

35. What are the team's strengths? How do we capitalize on them?

Comments: _____

_____

_____

CHAPTER 5

ENVIRONMENTAL INFLUENCES

The next step is to use the results of the team effectiveness questionnaire and the material in this chapter to resolve environmental issues.

> ***Process:***
> • Individually complete Force Field Analysis
> • Team discussion and problem solving
> • Complete Action Plan
> • Discuss recommendations with key managers

Team Environment

All teams operate within a larger environment, the organization and the outside world, that influences how they function. For example, the organization structure, policies, procedures, and systems can either support or hinder a team's effectiveness. The items listed below demonstrate how the key ingredients of an organization can support or hinder teamwork. For example, decision making by the team does not fit with an organization that restricts the information necessary for teams to make informed effective decisions.

MANAGEMENT PHILOSOPHY

Supportive:
• High involvement at all levels.

• Long term planning and results.

Hindering:
• Little involvement.
  Decisions at the top.
• Short term planning and results.

ORGANIZATION STRUCTURE

Supportive:
• Flat structure, few levels, decisions frequently made where problem occurs.

Hindering:
• Hierarchy with many levels, many approvals needed.

ORGANIZATION STRUCTURE (cont.)

Supportive:
- Organize teams according to work to be performed.

Hindering:
- Organized in ways inconsistent with work to be accomplished.

SYSTEMS

Supportive:
- Free flow of information to the team.
- Team rewards.
- Team goals.

Hindering:
- Information restricted by level.
- Individual rewards only.
- Individual goals only.

POLICIES

Supportive:
- Low status differentiation in the organization.
- All levels approachable.

Hindering:
- High status differentiation.

- Upper levels unapproachable.

SKILLS

Supportive:
- Teams receive training and experiences to develop job, interpersonal and leadership skills necessary to perform effectively.

Hindering:
- Little or no support for skill building.

Team Environment Task

Purpose: To determine the impact of the environment upon the team and to develop an action plan to reduce the impact of forces working against teamwork.

A helpful tool in identifying environmental influences that are supportive of or hindering teams is "Force Field Analysis" developed by Kurt Levin. This process helps the team examine the important outside influences and to develop plans to improve team performance.

Use the previous pages and the environment results of the Team Effectiveness Questionnaire to complete this task.

Principles of Force Field Analysis

The level of a team's effectiveness is held in a relatively steady state by a series of forces from opposing directions. There are supporting forces that work in favor of team effectiveness and hindering forces that work against.

Increasing supporting forces may move teamwork toward the new state, but frequently produces new or stronger counter or hindering forces.

The recommended strategy to improve teamwork is to reduce the impact of hindering forces. This helps the team move toward the new state without building further resistance or tension in the system.

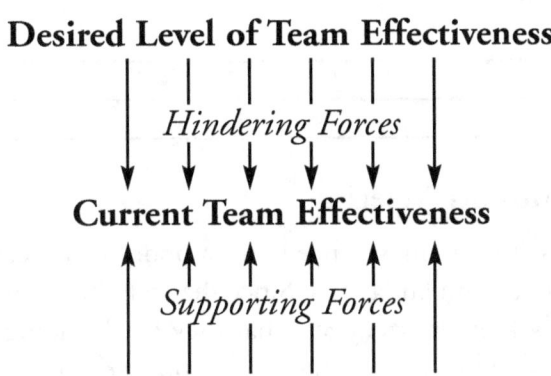

Desired Level of Team Effectiveness

Hindering Forces

Current Team Effectiveness

Supporting Forces

Instructions: *As a team, identify environmental forces, i.e., forces outside of the team, that are supporting and hindering team effectiveness, by drawing a force field on a flip chart. Specifically the team should:*

Identify and list on a flip chart forces working for teamwork

_____

_____

_____

Identify and list forces working against teamwork.

_____

_____

_____

Instructions: *Discuss how to improve the team's performance by reducing the impact of hindering forces. To start, pick a force - one that the team can influence and make progress on. Answer the following questions to develop an action plan.*

What is hindering this team's performance and how do we limit its impact?

_____

_____

_____

Who else needs to be involved to help resolve this issue and what role should they play in the resolution?

_____

_____

_____

Organizational Support Meeting

Schedule a meeting with whomever needs to support your recommendations, and review and discuss the recommendations. Since the team has given the subject considerable thought, don't ask other attendees what they think should be done before you make your recommendations, as they have probably spent little time on the subject and may have an answer that does not address the recommendations the team wishes to emphasize. It is important that they hear your points of view before they make decisions.

The meeting should be informal, and the presentation should be supported by a computer and screen or a flip chart. Dialogue should be encouraged. The result you want is to have everyone feeling that they are a part of the final decision. A brief evaluation at the end of the meeting with everyone giving their snapshot regarding their feelings about the outcome helps to identify loose ends and ensure satisfaction with the results.

Team Environment Action Plan

Instructions: *This space is for a written summary of actions to be taken, with responsibilities and follow-up dates. This document should also include dates for future meetings to discuss unresolved issues.*

Environmental Issue	Actions	Persons Responsible	Follow-up Dates
1.			
2.			
3.			
4.			
5.			
6.			

CHAPTER 6

TEAM GOALS

Use the results of the Team Effectiveness Questionnaire and the Goal Setting Task to resolve goal issues.

The establishment of individual goals has been the norm for most organizations. Yet the interdependent members of a team cannot accomplish their goals without the cooperation, services or resources of other members of the team.

Teams need to clearly identify what goals require teamwork and establish them as team goals with the commensurate joint accountability. Until this is done, there will always be win-lose competition for resources and no common goal to resolve it.

GOAL CHARACTERISTICS

The clarity of the goal and the extent to which it is understood and achievable depends upon how it is written.

A goal should have the following characteristics:
• A specific statement of what is to be accomplished with an action verb.
• The end result should be measurable.
• There should be a date for accomplishment.

Example: Increase production from 88% of capacity to 96% by April 4.

Team Goals Setting

Purpose: To identify, develop and clarify team goals and the members involved in their accomplishments.

A team exists when its members have responsibility for accomplishing a common goal.

For effective team functioning, it is important that the goals be clearly written and understood and that all team members are committed to their accomplishment.

Team members may have some goals that they can accomplish independently of the team. Other goals will require two or more members of the team to accomplish them and are "team goals." Differentiating between team and individual goals will help members better understand when they need to coordinate their activities.

A team goal should meet one or more of the following criteria.

TEAM GOAL CRITERIA

Requires a team or two or more members to accomplish

It is critical to the success or failure of the overall team mission.

Instructions: Individually list what you feel are the team's goals and who should be involved in accomplishing them. Each team member should explain their list while the others listen for understanding. Goals that appear on several lists do not have to be reviewed more than once. Ensure that all team members who contribute to the achievement of the goal are listed below it.

TEAM GOALS

1. Goal: _____

    Members Involved: _____

2. Goal: _____

    Members Involved: _____

3. Goal: _____

    Members Involved: _____

4. Goal: _____

   Members Involved: _____

5. Goal: _____

   Members Involved: _____

Instructions: *Upon reviewing each team member's list, discuss and reach consensus on the major team goals. They should be written below, with a statement of what is to be accomplished and by what date, and should be measurable.*

	Goal	**Accomplishment**	**Date**	**Measure**
1.				
2.				
3.				
4.				

Team Goals Action Plan

Instructions: This space is for a written summary of actions to be taken, with responsibilities and follow-up dates. This document should also include dates for future meetings to discuss unresolved issues.

Goal	Actions	Persons Responsible	Follow-up Dates
1. _____	_____	_____	_____
_____	_____	_____	_____
_____	_____	_____	_____
2. _____	_____	_____	_____
_____	_____	_____	_____
_____	_____	_____	_____
3. _____	_____	_____	_____
_____	_____	_____	_____
_____	_____	_____	_____
4. _____	_____	_____	_____
_____	_____	_____	_____
_____	_____	_____	_____
5. _____	_____	_____	_____
_____	_____	_____	_____
_____	_____	_____	_____
6. _____	_____	_____	_____
_____	_____	_____	_____
_____	_____	_____	_____

CHAPTER 7

ROLE CLARIFICATION

There are three tasks in this chapter designed to clarify roles. The first two tasks are combined. There is usually no need to do all three. Pick the one that best suits your team's needs. The first task, Job Responsibilities, is most useful when team members have clearly definable jobs. The second task, Role Mapping, is most useful when jobs are loosely defined, e.g. some are staff jobs, others are key management jobs.

Use these materials and the results of the Team Effectiveness Survey to resolve role issues.

> ***Process:***
> • Individually complete Job Responsibilities or Role Mapping
> • Team discussion of roles
> • Develop role action plan

Job Responsibilities

It is important that all team members understand what they and others are to do to accomplish the goals of the team. This task is intended to help each member of the team prepare a brief description of their job.

Purpose: To increase each team member's understanding of other's responsibilities and to clarify roles.

Instructions: *Each team member should list the major pieces of work for which they are responsible, answer the following questions and complete the team members' expectations task. Upon completion of both tasks, the results will be discussed as a team.*

Work	Responsibility
Example: *Operate the Number 2 Machine*	*Perform minor adjustments.* *Shut down if not producing quality.*

1. _____
_____

2. _____
_____

3. _____
_____

4. _____
_____

5. _____
_____

6. _____
_____

7. _____
_____

JOB RESPONSIBILITIES QUESTIONS

Identify work for which you are unclear about your responsibility or the responsibilities of others. Specify what needs clarification.

_____

_____

_____

_____

Identify responsibilities you believe overlap or conflict with those of other team members.

_____

_____

_____

_____

What, if anything, is unclear about the team's responsibility?

_____

_____

_____

_____

Identify team responsibilities that you believe are not being addressed or are falling through the cracks.

_____

_____

_____

_____

Team Member Expectations

As team members work together, they develop expectations of one another that are seldom recorded in job descriptions or other organizational documents. These expectations should be discussed and agreed upon, as they greatly determine team members' roles. For example: team member "A" expects "B" to help out when "A" is overloaded.

Purpose: To understand and clarify team members' expectations of each other.

Instructions:

Step 1. Individually identify what team members can expect of you and then what you expect of other team members.

Step 2. Discuss your responses as a team. Start with job responsibilities, then expectations, and have team member A present what their job is, their answers to the questions and what other team members can expect of him/her. Then each member should present their expectations of team member A. Continue until every team member's responsibilities and expectations are discussed and any necessary changes are identified.

What can team members expect of me?

_____

_____

_____

_____

What do I expect of other team members?

Team Member   **My Expectations**

_____

_____

_____

_____

Role Mapping

Role Mapping [4] examines how position in the organizational hierarchy and functional responsibilities shape ones role on the team. Its purpose is to diagram how team members interact. It should result in individual or group actions to change or clarify roles, expectations, and how team members interact. Each team member should draw a map depicting his role and explain it to the team.

Drawing Map

Each member of the team should individually draw a role map (on 26" or 32" flip chart paper, if available). The map should contain the names of the team members and those of people outside the team who have a significant impact on the performance of the team.

1. Draw circles of different sizes to represent the relative influence you feel the person has on decisions that have impact on the team. The larger the circle, the greater the influence.

2. Arrange distance between circles to represent the perceived amount of interdependence between you and others. The closer the circles to yours, the more interdependent you are with them.

3. Show lines with arrows of varying width to represent direction and amount of communication between you and others.

4. On a separate page, prepare a brief commentary or listing regarding the 3 to 5 major things you expect of each team member, and what they can expect of you.

5. Review your map and identify what you want to change or discuss regarding your role. The following questions may be helpful in this review.

   a.) Do you want to change:
      • Your communications with members of the team?
      • The amount of influence you have?

---

4 James H. Shonk. "Working in Teams," (New York: Amacom, 1982). Discussing Maps

> • The extent of interdependence with others?

b.) Are the expectations that others have of you the right expectations for optimal team performance?

c.) Is this the best role for you for the team's overall effectiveness?

After answering the preceding questions, each person should explain their map and present what others can expect of them. At that point, team members should add expectations from their list that have not been covered.

Team members may ask questions for understanding, but should hold items for discussion until the member presenting has completed their explanation. Discussion of issues or concerns that should be resolved by only a few members of the team should be noted on a flip chart and scheduled for a later time. Some subjects can be discussed and resolved immediately; others may take considerable time and should be held either until all members have reviewed their maps or at a later date.

When all maps have been explained and discussed, the total group should review and discuss the following questions.

1. Do team members' roles overlap? How should the overlaps be handled?

2. Are team members' roles in conflict? How should the conflict be resolved?

3. Are there differences between my expectations and the expectations of others?

4. What actions are indicated to improve how we function as a team?

Sample Role Map

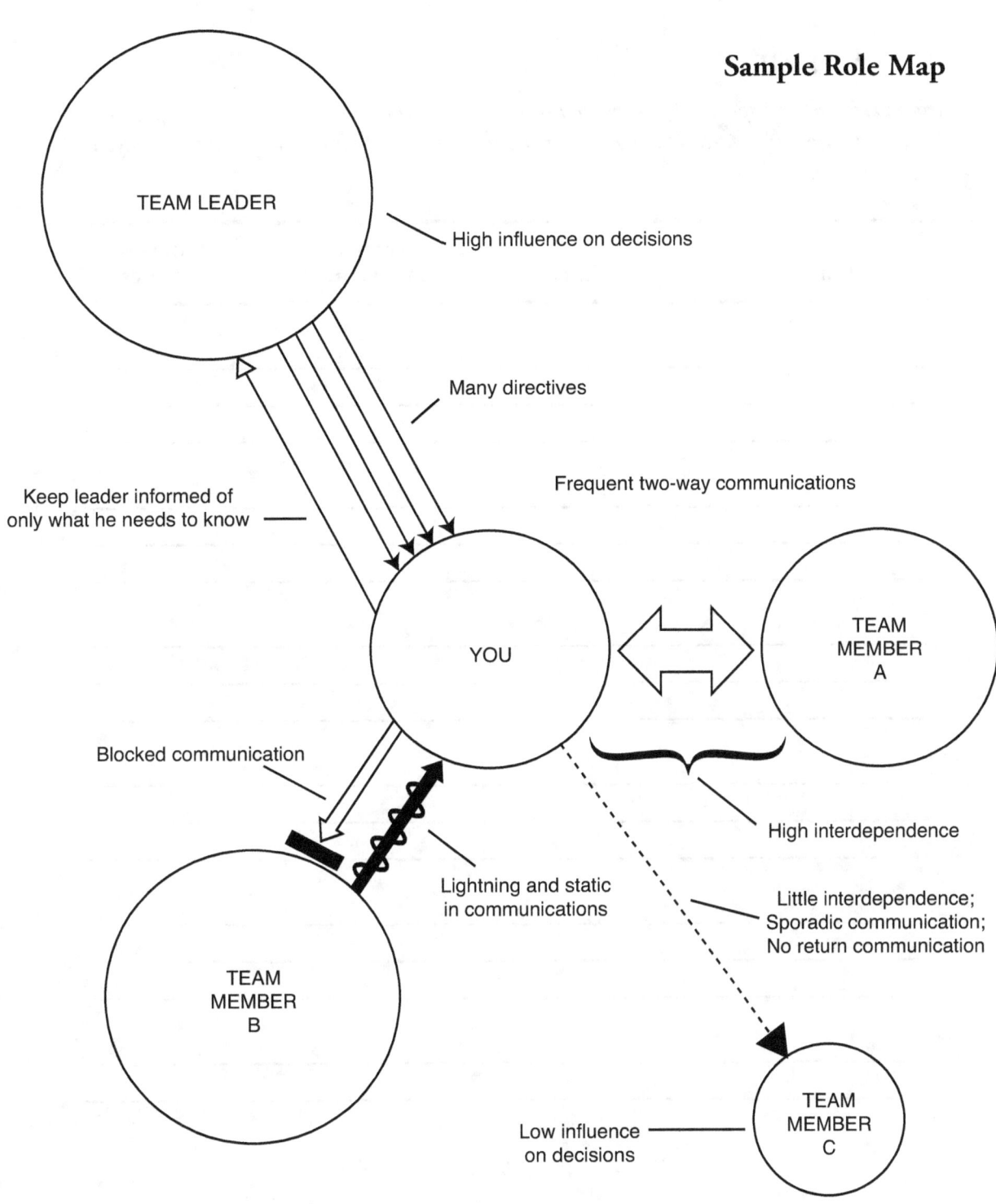

Roles Action Plan

Instructions: *This space is for a written summary of actions to be taken, with responsibilities, and follow-up dates. This document should also include dates for future meetings to discuss unresolved issues.*

	Role	Actions	Persons Responsible	Follow-up Dates
1.				
2.				
3.				
4.				
5.				
6.				

CHAPTER 8

TEAM DECISION MAKING

Process:
- Individually complete Decision Chart
- As a team determine how decisions will be made
- Determine Action Plans

INDIVIDUAL DECISION CRITERIA

1. The person had the knowledge to make the decision.

2. The decision falls within their area of responsibility.

3. The decision does not affect other team members.

TEAM DECISION CRITERIA

1. The knowledge needed to make the decision is distributed across several members of the team and the quality of the decision will be greatly improved by involving them.

2. Several members of the team will need to implement the decision and therefore need to understand and agree with it.

3. The decision will have impact on the work areas of several members of the team.

There are two factors to be considered in team decision making.

The quality of the decision
Is it the best decision, given the information and circumstances?

The acceptance of the decision

Will the people who are affected or have to implement the decision accept it?

The acceptance of the decision is a function of the person's involvement in the decision making process and their understanding of the rationale for the decision.

Consensus decision making

Consensus means that all team members have had the opportunity to share their views and explore options until the team reaches a decision that everyone is willing to support or accept. Team members may have a different opinion at first or even disagree with the decision. However, they must be willing to support the decision and complete their responsibilities once they have reached consensus.

Consensus tends to promote win-win relationships between team members and avoids win-lose situations that can split the team. Voting is typically a win-lose method and usually results in the dissatisfaction of the minority members, which naturally leads to lack of true commitment to the "team" decision. Voting often leads to the careless treatment of issues and decisions just to "get on with it." Compromise decision-making can have negative results also. Compromise requires that everyone give up something. Therefore, everyone losses a little and the final decision or solution may lose a lot.

Synergy

"Two heads are better than one." Team members pooling their abilities can accomplish much more than they are able to by working individually. All of the team's members bring different skills, knowledge, creative abilities, and experience to the team. This produces the capacity for creating more ideas. They promote "chain reactions" where ideas are sparked from other ideas which might not have occurred to one person working alone. Consequently, in most cases, the team is more capable than all of the separate individual team members working by themselves.

Team Decision Chart

Purpose: To identify team decisions and determine how they will be made.

Instructions: Complete the team decision chart for major team decisions. Using the team decisions criteria, identify team decisions and list them on the left-hand side of the matrix. Team members, or others, should be listed, and their method of involvement indicated with one of the symbols listed below. Also identify information that will be needed to make those decisions that the team does not now make. Select a leader, recorder and facilitator.

I = **Informed of the decision**
C = **Consulted before decision is made.**
D = **Decides. More than one (D) requires a consensus.**

Example:

Decision	People Involved and Method of Involvement			
	Supervisor	*Operator*	*Lab Tech*	*Receiving*
Reject sub-quality parts	*I*	*D*	*C*	*I*

Decision	People Involved and Method of Involvement			

Identify information needed to make these decisions.

_____

_____

_____

Are decisions being made by others that the team should be making?

_____

_____

_____

Team Decisions Action Plan

Instructions: *This space is for a written summary of actions to be taken, with responsibilities and follow-up dates. This document should also include dates for future meetings to discuss unresolved issues.*

	Decision	Actions	Persons Responsible	Follow-up Dates
1.				
2.				
3.				
4.				
5.				
6.				

CHAPTER 9

MEETINGS

Process:
- Individually complete agenda
- Agree on agenda
- Complete and discuss meeting evaluation
- Develop meeting action plan

Use the materials in this chapter plus the results of the team effectiveness questionnaire to improve team meetings. Team members frequently complain that they can't accomplish anything, because they are always attending meetings. Meetings should be looked upon as a way to accomplish the team's work. This requires that the team be clear what its work is and what can best be accomplished in a meeting and, importantly, what should not be done in team meetings.

Meeting Content

The meeting content consists of the agenda, materials and participants.

Meetings often continue longer than everyone would like because the leader and the participants have not identified in advance whether a meeting is really needed, who should attend, subjects to be covered, and what they wish to accomplish.

AGENDA FORMAT

Purpose: To plan an agenda for your team meetings.

Instructions: Using the following agenda format, create an agenda for either your regular team meetings or specifically for an upcoming meeting. First complete this agenda individually, then as a team agree on the agenda. Use a flip chart to record your agenda.

Agenda Example:

Meeting Title: *Weekly team meeting*

Date:

Starting Time: Ending Time:

Location:

Prework: *Read computer study*

Materials:

Subjects (no priority order)	Persons Responsible	Goals	Process	Time Allocated
Purchase computer system A or B	*Alice to answer questions regarding study*	*Decide which system to purchase*	*Q & A*	*30 min.*
1.				
2.				
3.				
4.				
5.				
6.				
7.				

Meeting Evaluation

One of the most effective methods for improving future meetings is to evaluate each meeting to determine what went well and should be continued, and what changes will improve the next meeting. The team should complete an evaluation after all meetings. Each person should briefly report what they feel the team did well and their suggestions for improvement. If there are some clear trends, the group should adopt the ideas for their next meeting.

Instructions: Individually complete an evaluation of the team's meeting and discuss the results as a team and how to improve future meetings.

PREPARATION	YES	NO
Was there adequate preparation for everyone to participate fully?	_____	_____

Comments: _____

_____

_____

AGENDA	YES	NO
Was there an agenda?	_____	_____
Did the team follow the agenda?	_____	_____
Did participants avoid topic jumping?	_____	_____

What subjects should be added to the next team meeting agenda?_____

_____

Comments: _____

_____

_____

GOAL	**YES**	**NO**
Were the meeting goals clearly stated and understood?	_____	_____
Was there agreement on the meeting goals?	_____	_____
Did the team accomplish its meeting goals?	_____	_____

Comments: _____
_____
_____

RESPONSIBILITIES	**YES**	**NO**
Was the leadership effective.	_____	_____
Was facilitation done effectively?	_____	_____
Was there a recorder?	_____	_____
Were ideas recorded and visible	_____	_____

Comments: _____
_____
_____

CONTENT	**YES**	**NO**
Were the materials and information distributed adequate?	_____	_____
Were the subjects discussed pertinent to the goals of the meeting?	_____	_____

Comments: _____
_____
_____

PARTICIPANTS	**YES**	**NO**
Were the right people in attendance?	_____	_____
Who else should have been included?	_____	_____

Comments: _____
_____
_____

PARTICIPATION	**YES**	**NO**
Did everyone participate?	_____	_____
Did we use the snapshot?	_____	_____

Comments: _____
_____
_____

LISTENING	**YES**	**NO**
Was there only one person talking at a time?	_____	_____
Did people listen and paraphrase for understanding?	_____	_____

Comments: _____
_____
_____

CONSENSUS	**YES**	**NO**
Did the team use Consensus Decision Making when needed?	_____	_____

Comments: _____
_____

FOLLOW-UP

	YES	NO

Have clear follow-up responsibilities been assigned?   _____   _____

Comments: _____

_____

_____

OTHER COMMENTS

_____

_____

_____

Meeting Action Plan

Instructions: This space is for a written summary of actions to be taken with responsibilities and follow-up dates. This document should also include dates for future meetings to discuss unresolved issues.

Meetings Issues	Actions	Persons Responsible	Follow-up Dates
1.			
2.			
3.			
4.			
5.			
6.			

CHAPTER 10

RESOLVING CONFLICT

Process:
- Individually Complete Team Norms
- Team Agree on Future Norms
- Develop Conflict Resolution Plan
- Complete and Discuss Team Spirit

Use the materials in this chapter, plus the results of the Team Effectiveness Questionnaire to resolve conflicts.

Team Behaviors

As teams work, norms or certain standards of behavior are established that are expected of team members. They can either help teamwork or hinder it.

HELPFUL BEHAVIORS	HINDERING BEHAVIORS
The team mission overrides individual goals.	Every person for herself/himself.
Mistakes surface rapidly.	Don't bring up bad news.
Problem solving is the top priority.	Look for scapegoats.

Helpful behaviors sustain high levels of team performance, while hindering behaviors hurt performance.

To reduce or eliminate the hindering behaviors it is necessary to understand why they exist and what reinforces their existence.

In most cases certain behaviors exist because they meet a need. Eliminating hindering behaviors requires addressing the cause and replacing them with helpful ones, or the team must find ways to reduce their negative impact. First it is necessary to identify what the behaviors are.

Team Behaviors Task

Purpose: To identify helpful and hindering behaviors and develop an action plan to either encourage or reduce each type of behavior.

Instructions: Each member of the team should complete the Helpful and Hindering Behaviors Task. The team should discuss each person's answers and reach consensus on actions to support helpful behaviors and reduce the impact of hindering behaviors.

List what you feel are existing helpful behaviors for the team.

HELPFUL BEHAVIORS

1. _____

2. _____

3. _____

4. _____

5. _____

Directions: *As a team, discuss your responses and reach agreement on the most significant hindering behaviors of the team and how to eliminate them or reduce their impact. List existing hindering behaviors and methods to reduce or eliminate them below.*

HINDERING BEHAVIORS	HOW TO ELIMINATE OR REDUCE IMPACT
1. _____	_____
2. _____	_____
3. _____	_____
4. _____	_____
5. _____	_____

Conflict Resolution

Instructions: *Individually identify what is causing conflict for the team by answering questions #1 & #2 below, and reach consensus on how to resolve or reduce the conflict.*

1. **What else is causing conflict within the team and how do we reduce or eliminate it?**

_____

_____

_____

2. **What outside groups or actions are causing conflict with the team and how do we we reduce or eliminate it?**

_____

_____

_____

Conflict Resolution Action Plan

Instructions: This space is for a written summary of actions to be taken, with responsibilities and follow-up dates. This document should also include dates for future meetings to discuss unresolved issues.

Conflict	Actions	Persons Responsible	Follow-up Dates

1._____

_____

_____

2._____

_____

_____

3._____

_____

_____

4._____

_____

_____

5._____

_____

_____

6._____

_____

Building Team Spirit

Purpose: To build team spirit and express how team members feel about what the team has accomplished.

Acknowledging the team's accomplishments is as important as discussing team problems. During this teamwork seminar the team has examined its performance and developed future plans to work more effectively. The team spirit activity is a celebration of your efforts and accomplishments. It should be used periodically to focus on accomplishments and build team spirit.

Instructions: Team members should individually review their experience during the teamwork meetings by answering the following questions. Each team member will then have an opportunity to express their comments on each question.

What do you feel the team has accomplished?

_____

_____

_____

_____

What do you feel good about regarding how this team functions?

_____

_____

_____

_____

Other Comments

_____

_____

_____

_____

CHAPTER 11

FOLLOW UP

Check-Up Meeting

This meeting should be held 3-6 months after the team completes its team building meetings.

Purpose: To maintain a high level of team effectiveness by periodically assessing team performance and developing plans for continuous improvement.

Continual examination of how well the team is doing, and determining how it can improve are prime factors in the continued high performance of a team. Periodically, the team should step back from its daily tasks to celebrate it's accomplishments and to improve performance. Such a meeting might happen quarterly, but certainly no less frequently than once a year. Done well, such a meeting can serve to recharge team members and recommit the team to excellence.

Team Effectiveness Questionnaire

Instructions: To prepare for this meeting, team members should complete the following questionnaire, and identify the top three priority items for discussion. Depending upon the number of subjects to be discussed, two hours to 1 day should be set aside for this meeting, Team members should come prepared to discuss their responses to the questionnaire and their three top priorities for team improvement. The focus of the meeting will be to develop appropriate action plans. "No" responses are areas for team discussion and the development of plans for improvement.

ENVIRONMENT	YES	NO
1. The team is adequately managing outside influences.	———	———
2. The organization is adequately supporting the team.	———	———
3. Outside influences are positively affecting team performance.	———	———

Comments: _____

_____

_____

GOALS	YES	NO
4. The team's mission is clear and agreed upon.	———	———
5. Team goals are clear, measurable and agreed upon.	———	———
6. Team members' goals are not in conflict.	———	———
7. Team members are committed to the team's goals.	———	———
8. The team's direction and focus of attention are consistent.	———	———

Comments: _____

_____

_____

ROLES	YES	NO
9. Team members' roles are clear and agreed upon.	———	———
10. Team members' roles are not in conflict.	———	———
11. Team members are performing their roles effectively.	———	———

ROLES (cont.)	**YES**	**NO**
12. There is effective use of team members' skills.	———	———
13. Assignments are finished on time.	———	———
14. The leader's role is effective for optimum team performance.	———	———

Comments: _____

_____

_____

PROCESSES	**YES**	**NO**
15. Decision making authority and the processes are clear.	———	———
16. The team uses consensus decision making when appropriate.	———	———
17. Decisions are made within the time deadlines.	———	———
18. The team consistently uses open dialogue and feedback.	———	———
19. The team receives the information it needs.	———	———
20. Team members are practicing active listening.	———	———
21. All meetings have an agenda.	———	———
22. All member participate in meetings.	———	———
23. Meetings consistently follow the agenda.	———	———
24. Meeting guidelines are followed.	———	———
25. Meetings are effective and cover relevant topics.	———	———

26. Meeting preparation and follow-up are consistently done.   ——— ———

27. Meetings are evaluated and improvements implemented.   ——— ———

28. Everyone who is needed at specific meetings always attends.   ——— ———

29. A clear plan exists for continually improving performance.   ——— ———

Comments: _____

_____

_____

RELATIONSHIPS   **YES**   **NO**

30. Relationships among team members are optimum.   ——— ———

31. conflicts are quickly surfaced and resolved.   ——— ———

General

32. What is causing stress for the team? _____

_____

_____

33. What will increase the effectiveness of this team? _____

_____

_____

34. What are the teams' strengths? How do we capitalize on them? _____

_____

_____

Check-Up Action Plans

Instructions: As the team discusses each member's answers, record agreed upon plans to improve team performance.

Action Steps	Persons Responsible	Follow-up Dates
1.		
2.		
3.		
4.		
5.		
6.		

Continued Team Building

The best efforts at developing a team are of little value if there is no follow-up on a day-to-day basis. The agreements the team reaches need to be implemented, which can be accomplished only when responsibilities are clear and people are held accountable. Team development is not something that happens only when the team meets. It is a day-to-day activity - a way of life.

The more opportunities the team can find to reinforce the changes decided upon, the greater the chances are that that change will be realized. Team development is no different from any other process within the organization. It requires reinforcement, supporting systems, and most of all, the team's commitment to make it work.

The Author:

James H. Shonk is the President of Shonk & Associates. He specializes in building teams, designing team-based organizations and rapidly adapting organizations and working with internal consulting groups to develop strategies for change.

Prior to forming Shonk & Associates, he was Manager of Organization Development for General Foods Corporation and held positions in Personnel and Organization Development with Exxon. His clients include many Fortune 500 companies.

Shonk holds an M.S. in Industrial Relations from The University of Wisconsin. In addition to his best-selling books on teams, he is a contributing author to *"Organization Development in Health Care"*. His article, *"What Business Teams Can Learn from Athletic Teams"*, appeared in *Personnel Magazine*. Mr. Shonk has also presented team concepts at The University of Michigan, The University of Connecticut, The National Training Laboratories and The Organization Development Network.

www.ingramcontent.com/pod-product-compliance
Lightning Source LLC
Chambersburg PA
CBHW081217170526
45165CB00009B/2847

9781453859407